The Best of Notice Board Gems?

(A few comments on Realities of Life)

COLLECTED and COMPILED

by

Brian A Lee-Blackmore
Les Yeoman
Paul Allington
Steve Gillard
&
Others

PLAYGROUND PUBLISHING

God grant me the courage to change the things I can.
The serenity to accept the things I cannot change
and the wisdom to know the difference.

Published by:

Playground Publishing

P.O. Box 125, Portsmouth
Hampshire. PO14PP
023 92 819162

ISBN 0-9535987-2-1

Illustrations by Willy Sanker

Printed and bound in Great Britain

THINK AHEAD

FOR SERVICE

RING BELL
WHISTLE
SHOUT
SCREAM
WHIMPER
BEG
THREATEN
GROVEL
WHINE

IF NONE OF THE ABOVE WORKS,

GO AWAY

ATTENTION ALL EMPLOYEES

— TO SAVE TIME, PLEASE GIVE EXCUSES BY THE NUMBER —

1. *The computer fouled it up.*
2. *I didn't think it was that important.*
3. *Don't blame me. I was hired for my looks.*
4. *That's not my department.*
5. *No one told me to go ahead.*
6. *I've been too busy.*
7. *We've always done it that way.*
8. *I forgot.*
9. *I was waiting for an O.K.*
10. *That's someone else's job.*
11. *The boss didn't tell me.*
12. *Sorry, I goofed.*

THE OPPOSITION OF INANIMATE OBJECTS

This phenomenon has been recognised as invariably variable.

It concerns the axiomatic observation that there is a high probability that highly unfavourable and improbable events will happen frequently.

The improbability of each discrete event is not reduced but it is clear that they occur too often for there not to be a perverse or malevolent propensity involved.

The definitive statement of this tendency is given as Murph's Law (otherwise known as Fingles 3rd Law or Sod's Law - after Eramus Upoor Sod; b. 1768 - d 1799 & 1800).

The Law has been generalised as THE LAW OF CONTINUOUS MISERY and is elegantly stated in Sod's final revelation of his own predicament:

ANYTHING THAT CAN GO WRONG INVARIABLY WILL.

Most students familiar with probability theory and critical path analysis will realise that there is little truth in the

A TREE is a plant that grows in the same spot for 50 years and then suddenly jumps in front of a Women Driver!

RIPOFF MOTORS PLC.

NOTICE – WORK COMPLETION.

Should mechanics be asked by customers as to when they expect to complete car repairs, the 'Official Replies List' must be used. The words 'soon', 'X hours, 'now' are prohibited. Permissible replies are 'I don't know', 'When we get the parts' or 'They don't make parts for this anymore'. A sharp intake of breath is allowed under aggressive questioning or extreme duress. It is unfair to customers to have their hopes raised and then to find that the car is actually ready on time. This phenomenon has been carefully researched.

Customers expect to wait at least 72 hours over and above any reasonable time for repairs; early returns can be traumatic. Most of you will know Mr Thomas – we took in his Wolseley 6/110 in 1967 and he tells us that he looks forward to his daily visits here. He amuses us with his tall stories of two occasions when he detected work being done on the car.

There is, of course, a small element amongst the general run of customers who can only be described as difficult. Not only do they create trouble if repairs are over long, but they expect to have repairs done safely and correctly!

Staff should consider this as part of the job and accept that there is little that can be done to remedy it. This kind of attitude is, fortunately, getting rarer.

When, and if, a car is handed back, the customer must sign the Liability Release Form which absolves the company from any responsibility or risk. It is at this time that 'final checks' can be made (out of view of the customer) and 'knock' and 'clunk' modifications can be introduced into the vehicle to ensure the customer comes back. This improves customer contact and gives the recovery truck steady business.

Oxygen and resuscitation equipment is now in operation in the 'Bill Presentation Room'. So far, only two customers have suffered cardiac arrest, following the 100% increase in labour charges, but this is expected to be reduced when the 'Second Mortgage Department' opens in June. The recent bad press that the motor trade has received recently (on the subject of charges) raises the question of accurate recording of overhead costs. From now on, 'customers' vehicles secretly used by the taxi division of our firm, will render the customer liable to charges if said customers vehicle breaks down while in service. Such additional costs (such as compensation for a staff member who misses a weekend at the casino because the customer's car fails to start) will be included in the bill presented to the customer when collecting their car.

Finally, staff are reminded of some 'gratitude' phrases such as: "I worked through the night on this"-, "-sifted for six hours in the scrap yard to find you this part"! and "This is the last time you'll see one of these, but here's my phone number, I might be able to get you one". As a rule, this may mean anything up to 50% on the official bill (now and later) and provides workshop staff with the possibility of alternative income.

N.B The customer, who kidnapped Mr. Roberts our Reception Manager and threatened to dismantle him unless he got his car back, has been told to go ahead.

Signed,
Work Duty Foreman
P.G.Lark.

I really trust my MECHANIC!

RUSH JOB CALENDAR

MIR	FRI	FRI	FRI	THU	WED	TUE
8	7	6	5	4	3	2
16	14	13	12	11	10	9
23	22	21	20	19	18	17
32	29	28	27	26	25	24
39	38	37	36	35	34	33

1. THIS IS A SPECIAL CALENDAR WHICH HAS BEEN DEVELOPED FOR   HANDLING RUSH JOBS. ALL RUSH JOBS ARE WANTED YESTERDAY. WITH THIS CALENDAR A CLIENT CAN ORDER WORK ON THE 7TH AND HAVE IT DELIVERED ON THE 3RD.

2. EVERYONE WANTS HIS JOB BY FRIDAY SO THERE ARE THREE FRIDAYS IN EVERYWEEK.

3. THERE ARE EIGHT NEW DAYS AT THE END OF THE MONTH FOR THOSE END OF THE MONTH JOBS.

4. THERE IS NO 1ST OF THE MONTH SO THERE CAN'T BE LATE DELIVERY OF END OF THE MONTH JOBS ON THE 1ST.

5. A "BLUE MONDAY" OR " MONDAY MORNING HANGOVER" CAN'T HAPPEN AS ALL MONDAYS HAVE BEEN ELIMINATED.

6. THERE ARE NO BOTHERSOME NON-PRODUCTIVE SATURDAYS AND SUNDAYS, COMPENSATORY LEAVE OR OVERTIME TO WORRY ABOUT.

7. WITH NO 15TH, 30TH OR 31ST, NO "TIME OFF" IS NECESSARY FOR CASHING SALARY CHEQUE EITHER.

8. "MIRDAY" - A SPECIAL DAY EACH WEEK FOR PERFORMING MIRACLES.

YOU WANT IT WHEN?!!!?

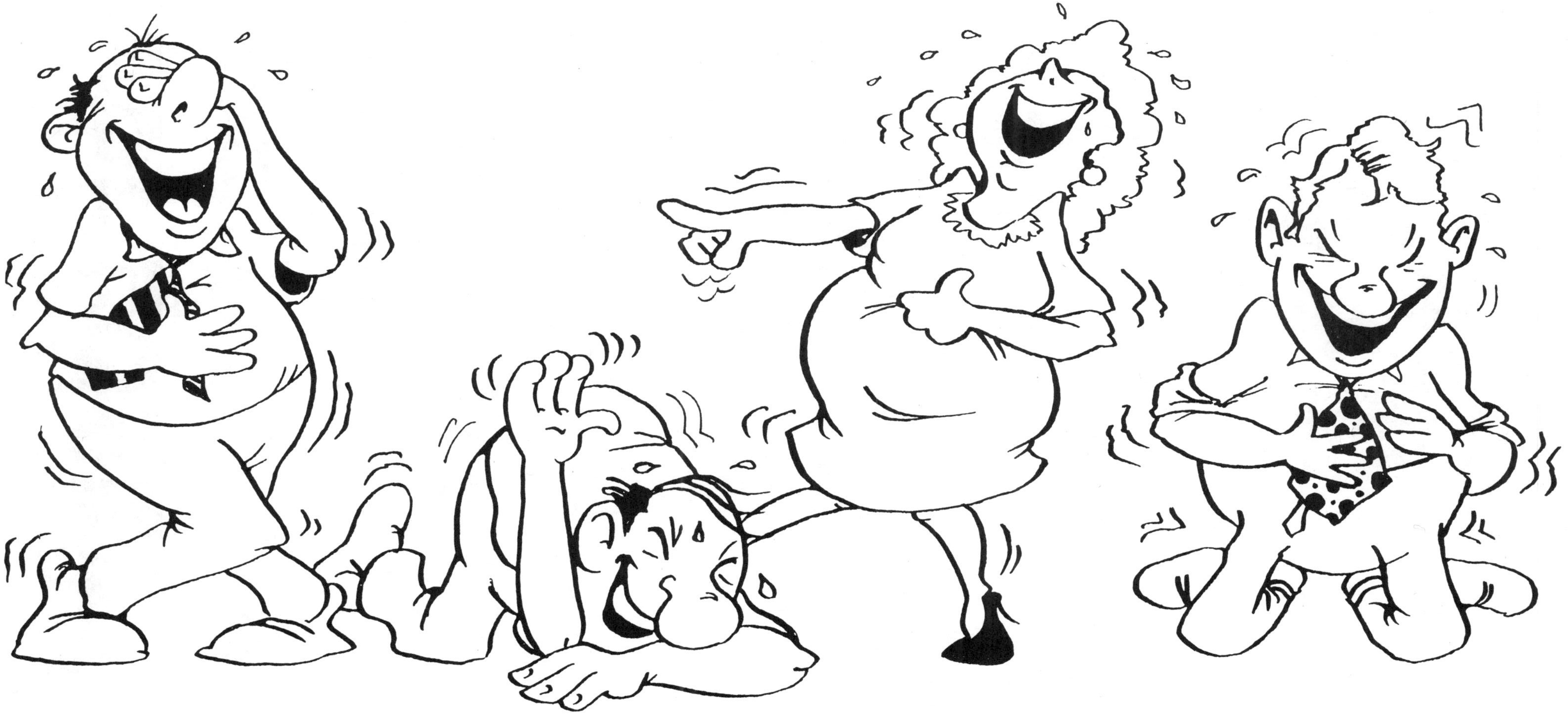

WIN or LOSE?

A winner says, "Let's find out".
A loser says, "Nobody knows."

When a winner makes a mistake, he says, "I was wrong."
When a loser makes a mistake, he says, "It wasn't my fault."

A winner works harder than a loser and has more time.
A loser is always "too busy" to do what is necessary.

A winner goes through a problem.
A loser goes around it and never gets past it.

A winner make commitments.
A loser makes promises.

A winner says, "I'm not as good as I ought to be."
A loser says, "I'm not as bad as a lot of other people."

A winner listens.
A loser explains away.

A winner feels responsibility for more than his job.
A loser says, "I only work here."

A winner says, "There ought to be a better way to do it."
A loser says, "That's the way it's always been done before."

A winner paces himself.
A loser has only two speeds - hysterical and lethargic.

Being a winner doesn't come easy.
Being a loser requires no work.

And remember that everybody knows "common sense".
- a loser just says "It's obvious".
- a winner actually does it.

A collection of newspaper headlines from around the world.

Red Tape Holds Up New Bridge

Man Struck by Lightning Faces Battery Charge

Is There a Ring of Debris Around Uranus

Cold Wave Linked
To Temperatures

Eye Drops Off Shelf

Astronaught Takes Blame
for Gas in Spacecraft

**Kids
Make
Nutritious
Snacks**

**Typhoon Rips Through
Cemetery, Hundreds Dead**

Teacher Strikes
Idle Kids

**Enraged Cow Injures
Farmer with Axe**

Iraqi Head Seeks Arms

Two Sisters Reunited
after 18 Years in
Checkout Counter

*Survivor of
Siamese Twins
Joins Parents*

Stolen Painting
Found by Tree

Regan Wins on Budget, But More Lies Ahead

Something Went Wrong in Jet Crash, Expert Says

If Strike isn't Settled Quickly, It May Last a While

**New Study
in Obesity
Looks For
Larger Test Group**

Miners Refuse to Work After Death

War Dims Hope
for Peace

Plane to Close to Ground, Crash Probe Told

British Union
Finds Dwarfs
in Short Supply

FOR SALE

BY OWNER, COMPLETE SET
ENCYCLOPEDIA BRITANNICA
EXCELLENT CONDITION
NO LONGER NEEDED
DEAREST WIFE
KNOWS EVERYTHING!

THE RULES

The **FEMALE** always makes The Rules.
The Rules are subject to change at
any time without prior notification.

No **MALE** can possibly know all The Rules.

If the **FEMALE** suspects the **MALE** knows
all The Rules she must immediately
change some or all of The Rules.

The Female is never wrong.

If The **FEMALE** is wrong it is due to a
misunderstanding which was a direct result of
something the **MALE** did or said wrong.

The **MALE** must apologise immediately
for causing said misunderstanding.

The **FEMALE** may change her mind at any time.

The **MALE** must never change his mind without
the express consent of the **FEMALE**.

The **FEMALE** has every right to
be angry or upset at any time.

The **MALE** must remain calm at all times, unless
the **FEMALE** wants him to be angry or upset.

The **FEMALE** must, under no circumstances,
let the **MALE** know whether or not she
wants him to be angry and/or upset.

The **MALE** is expected to mind read at all times.

The **MALE** who does not abide by The Rules cannot
take the heat, lacks backbone and is a wimp.

Any attempt to document The Rules
could result in bodily harm.

It the **FEMALE** has PMT all The Rules are null and void.

The **FEMALE** is ready when she is ready.

The **MALE** must be ready at all times.

WATCH IT!

This is a bad day. I'm feeling very fragile.
Speak to me quietly in dulcet tones and let
not one offensive word be uttered.
Take care to move slowly (for my vision is
impaired and sudden movement may
alarm me). Be aware that I have occupied
this desk for **20** years and it pains me to
know that here I will stay for another **20** years.
Tread softly then, and show respect
and reverence for someone of mature
years and gentle disposition – or
I'll get up and beat the living daylights out of you.

GOD I LOVE THIS PLACE...

PLEASE BE PATIENT, I ONLY WORK HERE BECAUSE I AM TOO OLD FOR A PAPER ROUTE, TOO YOUNG FOR SOCIAL SECURITY AND TOO TIRED TO HAVE AN AFFAIR.

SECRETARY BURNOUT

HAIR FRIZZLED
FROM BAD NERVES

HARD OF HEARING
FROM EXPOSURE TO
TELEPHONE AND
DICTAPHONE

BAD EYESIGHT
FROM DECIPHERING
POOR HANDWRITING

PERMANENT WRINKLES
FROM CONSTANT SMILE
AND DEADLINE PRESSURE

BAD POSTURE FROM
BENDING OVER DESK

TACKY CLOTHES
FROM 25 YEARS
OF LOW PAY

ULCER FROM
HOLDING BACK
URGE TO PUNCH
SOMEBODY

HAND LOST
IN PHOTOCOPYING
MACHINE

FINGER CANCER
FROM TOO MANY
REWRITES, RETYPES
AND PAPER CUTS

TENNIS SHOE
TOE FROM
COFFEE TRIPS

HOW TO BE LOVED BY YOUR SECRETARY

1. NEVER start work first thing in the morning – we much prefer a terrific rush in the afternoon.

2. Please smoke when dictating: it assist's pronunciation.

3. Do not face us when dictating: this would be too easy for us.

4. Hours for dictating: During the lunch hour or any time between 4.30 and 5.30 p.m.

5. When dictating, please parade up and down the room. We can understand what is said more distinctly.

6. Please call us in for dictation and then proceed to sort out papers, look up old files, telephone and receive calls etc.

7. Please lower the voice to whisper when dictating names of people, places etc. and under no circumstances spell them out to us. We are sure to hit upon the right way of spelling them. We know the name and address of every person, firm and place in the world.

8. When we do not hear a word and dictators are asked to repeat it, shout it as loud as possible. We find this more gentlemanly. Alternatively, dictators should refuse to repeat it at all. We have second sight and it may come to us.

9. Whenever possible, dictators should endeavour to keep us late. We have no homes and are only too thankful for somewhere to spend the evening.

10. Should a letter require slight alteration after it is typed, score the word heavily through about four times and write the correct word beside it, preferably in ink or heavy pencil, and always make the alteration on the top copy.

11. Should we be too busy, or too lazy, to take down dictation, please write letters with a blunt pencil in the left hand, whilst blindfolded. Incorrect spellings, balloons, arrows and other diagrams are very helpful to us.

12. With regard to statements, do not on any account use lined paper. If figures are altered, please write heavily over those previously inserted, the correct figure in each case being the one underneath.

13. Should work be required urgently (a most unusual occurrence) it aids us considerably if you rush in at intervals of 30 seconds to see if it is done.

14. If extra copies of a letter are required, this desire should be indicated either after "Yours faithfully", or overleaf, so as to ensure that it is the last thing the typist see's when the letter is completed.

15. When we stagger out carrying a pile of files, please do not open the door for us; we learn to open it with our teeth, or crawl under it.

DON'T CRITICISE THE STANDARD OF WORK IN THIS OFFICE - THE MESS AND CONFUSION IS NOTHING COMPARED TO WHAT IT WOULD BE IF YOU WERE HANDLING IT.

EVERYTHING IS POSSIBLE AND MAY BE ACCOMPLISHED WITH EASE SO LONG AS IT'S NOT YOU THAT HAS TO DO IT!

I COULD BE VERY DECISIVE IF ONLY SOMEONE WOULD TELL ME WHAT TO DO!

I'VE JUST HAD ONE OF THOSE DAY'S WHEN I DID EVERYTHING ABSOLUTELY RIGHT - WHY WEREN'T YOU HERE TO SEE IT?

A
ROUND TWIT

....

At long last we have a sufficient quantity for each of you to have your own. These tuits have been hard to come by, especially the round ones. This is an indispensable item. It will help you become a much more efficient worker. For years we have heard people say: "I'll do this as soon as I get a round tuit". Now that you have a round tuit of your own, many things that have been needing to be accomplished will get done.....

a round twit a round twit a round twit a round twit a round twit a round twit a round twit a round twit a round twit a round twit a round twit a round twit a round twit

January 15,

Mr Fred Glomph
Sales Manager
Fly-By-Night Gizmo Co.
25 Seedy Street
Cavveat Emtorville

Dear Mr Glomph,

Your "EVERLAST" dining set lasted only 3 days. It disintegrated.

Not only that, but the remains of it dissolved my table, fell on the floor and caused extensive discoloration. And Aunt Maude, while cleaning it up, got some on her hands and immediately fell into a fit. While she was thrashing around on the floor, she kicked our wee son Mortimer in the eye and he, too, is in the hospital. In our rush to take these two casualties to the hospital, my wife left a cigarette burning in the living room and, upon our return, we discovered that our house had burned down. Seeing this and realizing that our insurance had run out, my poor wife, distraught, wandered into the road and she was struck down by a passing bus...number 49, if I recall.

Legal consultation has brought to light the fact that you have covered yourself totally and will assume no responsibility whatsoever for my predicament. Therefore I am sure you will understand fully when I tell you that the paper in this letter has been saturated with Anthrax 46, a fast-acting nerve toxin which has no known antidote. Just touching the paper is enough to give you a lethal dose.

Before the convulsions begin, I hope you will authorize the replacement "EVERLAST" dining set to which I am entitled under your warranty. *After all there is no sense in bearing a grudge.*

Sincerely,
Wadsworth Wort

THE SUPERMARKETS
Have you ever wondered why...

- Have you ever wondered why in any supermarket the number of check - out operators reduces as the number of customers trying to get out increases.

- Why flour bags have the bottom flap glued with less than the minimum of adhesive - the top flap needs a locomotive to tear it away ?

- Why trolley carts are never stacked, they are permanently interlocked or welded together ? If you do find one that which is free, it's got bidirectional wheels.

- Why anything worth a special trip to the supermarket has just sold out ?

- Why what's brilliant white inside the supermarket is a dull yuk when seen in daylight ?

- Why whatever you get to like this month will be discontinued through 'lack of consumer interest' next month ?

- Why we continue to fall for the same old 'Sales and Marketing' tricks they conjure up ?

"Those pills you gave me don't seem to be helping much Doctor – it's been two weeks now and I'm the same as if I hadn't taken them."

"On the contrary, if you hadn't taken them you'd be dead by now."

SELF CERTIFICATION FORM
(OFFICIAL)

APPLICATION TO BE ILL

This form must be submitted at least 21 days before the date on which you wish illness to commence.

NAME .... CLOCK/EMPLOYEE NO ....

DEPARTMENT .... POSITION HELD ....

NATURE OF ILLNESS ....

DATE ON WHICH ILLNESS TO COMMENCE ....

(Applications to suffer from Pregnancy must be submitted 12 months prior, and accompanied by from no. WS.36/24/36. Consent of Husband/Wife ....

HAVE YOU EVER APPLIED TO SUFFER FROM THIS ILLNESS BEFORE ....

IF YES, GIVE DATE ....

DO YOU WISH ILLNESS TO BE SLIGHT/SEVERE/CRIPPLING/FATAL ....

DO YOU WISH TO SUFFER THIS ILLNESS AT HOME/HOSPITAL/COSTA BRAVA/FLORIDA OR BOGNOR REGIS ....

DO YOU WISH THIS ILLNESS TO BE OF A CONTAGIOUS NATURE ....

IF YES, INDICATE APPROXIMATE NUMBER OF PEOPLE YOU WISH TO INFECT ....

HAVE YOU EVER BEEN REFUSED PERMISSION TO SUFFER FROM AN ILLNESS, IF YES, PLEASE GIVE DETAILS ....

DO YOU WISH YOUR WIFE/HUSBAND TO BE INFORMED OF YOUR ILLNESS IF SHE/HE SHOULD CONTACT THE COMPANY REGARDING YOUR WHEREABOUTS ....

I, the undersigned, declare that to the best of my knowledge the answers given above are true and accurate.

Signed .... Date ....

Applicants are reminded that all requests are considered on merit and more than three applications per annum will be considered excessive and not in the best interests of the Company. Under NO CIRCUMSTANCES will permission be given for more than one fatal illness per applicant.

SIX PHASES OF A PROJECT

1   ENTHUSIASM

2   DISILLUSIONMENT

3   PANIC

4   SEARCH FOR THE GUILTY

5   PUNISHMENT OF THE INNOCENT

6   PRAISE & HONOURS FOR THE NON-PARTICIPANTS

Those of you who think you know everything are very annoying to those of us who do.

The strongest drive is not sex or greed. It is one person's need to change another's copy.

amend

change another's

copy.

alter

reshape

qualify

modify.......

stat

revise

transform

improve

rewrite

I, THE WILLING,

LED BY THE IGNORANT,

AM DOING THE IMPOSSIBLE,

FOR THE UNGRATEFUL.

I HAVE DONE SO MUCH,

FOR SO LONG,

WITH SO LITTLE,

THAT I AM NOW HIGHLY QUALIFIED,

TO DO ANYTHING,

WITH NOTHING!

How to tell a Businessman from a Businesswoman

A businessman is aggressive;
a businesswoman is pushy.

He is careful about details;
she is picky.

He loses his temper because
he's so involved in his job;
she's bitchy.

He's depressed (or hung over),
so everyone tiptoes past his office;
she's moody, so it must be
her time of the month.

He follows through;
she doesn't know when to quit.

He's firm;
she's stubborn.

He makes wise judgements;
she reveals her prejudices.

He is a man of the world;
she's been around.

He isn't afraid to say what he thinks;
she's opinionated.

He exercises authority;
she's tyrannical.

He's discreet;
she's secretive.
He's a stern taskmaster;
she's difficult to work for.

MEMORANDUM

To: All employees
From: Personal Department
Subject: Excessive Absences

Due to the excessive number of absences from the office the following rules and procedures will be put into effect as of this instant.

SICKNESS:
No excuse. We will no longer accept your doctor's statement as proof, as we believe if you are able to go to the doctor you are able to come to work.

DEATH:
(Other than your own) this is no excuse. There is nothing you can do for them and we are sure that someone else with a lesser position can attend to the arrangements. However, if the funeral can be held in the late afternoon, we will be glad to let you off one hour early, providing that your share of the work is ahead enough to keep the job going in your absence.

LEAVE OF ABSENCE:
(For an operation) we are no longer allowing this practice. We wish to discourage any thoughts that you need an operation. We believe as long as you are an employee here, you will need all of whatever you have and you should not consider having anything removed. We hired you as you are and to have anything removed would certainly make you less than we bargained for.

DEATH:
(Your own) this will be accepted as an excuse but we would like a two week notice, as we feel it is your duty to teach someone else your job.

ALSO:
Entirely too much time is being spent in the restroom. In the future we will follow this practice of going in alphabetical order. For instance, those with names beginning with "A" will go from 8.00 to 8.15; "B" will go from 8.15 to 8.30, and so on. If you are unable to go at your appointed time, *it will be necessary to wait until the next day when your time comes again.*

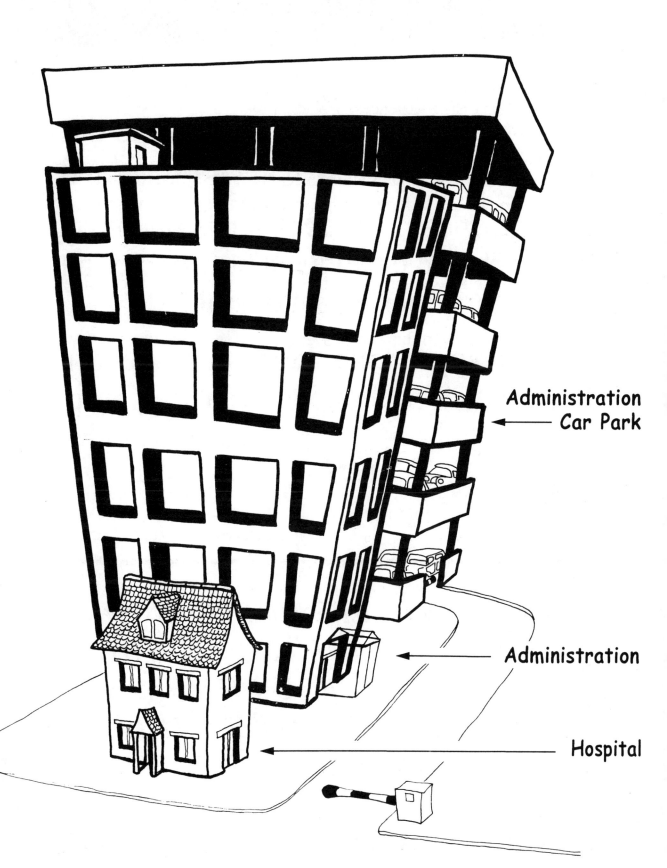

Administration
Car Park

Administration

Hospital

STAFF NOTICE

Management notes that employees dying on the job are failing to fall down.

This practice must cease, it is becoming impossible to distinguish between death and natural movement of staff.

Any employee found dead in an upright position will be dropped from the payroll.

By Order.

C.E.O.

DUE TO THE PRESENT ECONOMIC SITUATION THE LIGHT AT THE END OF THE TUNNEL HAS BEEN TURNED OFF UNTIL FURTHER NOTICE.

THE FLOGGINGS AND HANGINGS WILL CONTINUE UNTIL MORALE IMPROVES

NOTICE

This department requires no physical fitness programme.

Everyone get enough exercise jumping to conclusions, flying off the handle, running down the boss, knifing people in the back, dodging responsibility, pushing their luck and passing the buck.

All the extracts given below are from genuine letters sent to the pensions office. Although crude they are written in good faith by the authors......

1. I cannot get sick pay, I have six children. Can you tell me why this is?

2. This is my eighth child. What are you going to do about it?

3. I am forwarding my marriage certificate and two children, one of which is a mistake as you can see.

4. Sir, I am glad to say that my husband, reported missing, is now dead.

5. I am writing these lines for Mrs G. who expects to be confined next week and can do with it.

6. I am sending you my marriage certificate and six children, I had seven and one died, which was baptised on half a sheet of paper by the Rev. Thomas.

7. In answer to your letter, I have given birth to a little boy weighing ten pounds. Is this satisfactory?

8. You have changed my little girl into a little boy, will this make any difference?

9. Please send my money at once as I have fallen into errors with my landlord.

10. In accordance with your instructions I have given birth to twins in the enclosed envelope.

11. Milk is wanted for my baby as the father is unable to supply it.

12. Re. your enquiry, the teeth in the top are alright but the ones in my bottom are hurting horribly.

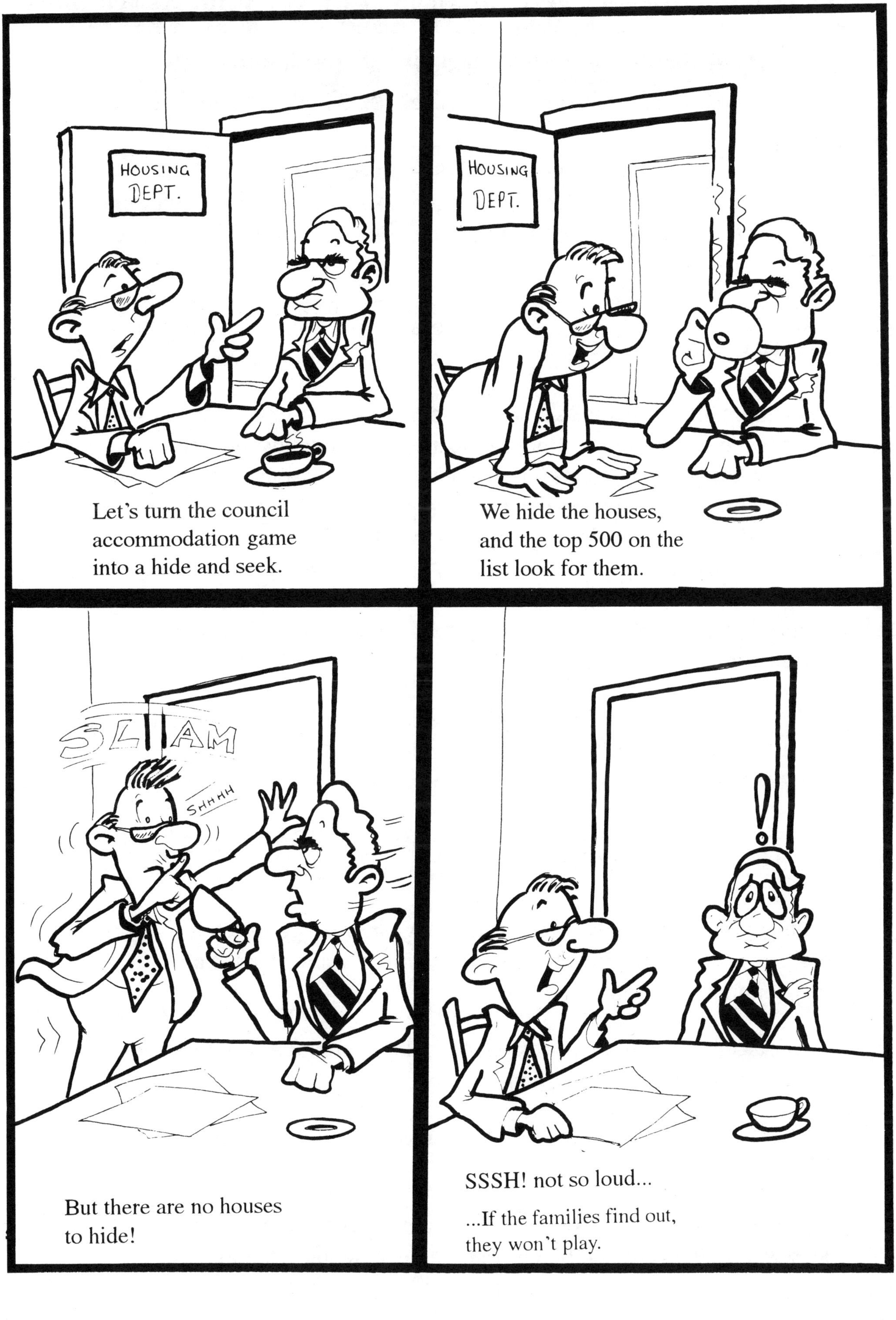
HOUSING DEPT.
Let's turn the council accommodation game into a hide and seek.
HOUSING DEPT.
We hide the houses, and the top 500 on the list look for them.
SLAM
SHHHH
But there are no houses to hide!
!
SSSH! not so loud...
...If the families find out, they won't play.

BASIC RULES ON HOW TO HELP YOUR SERVICE ENGINEER

1 Never send for him until everyone in the office has had time to form their own opinion as to what is wrong and how to fix it. (have a different operator available and make sure only he/she has no idea what happened or why).

2 After sending for the engineer move every desk, table and waste box into the room, thereby making sure he can't get to the machine.

3 The moment he arrives ask him where he has been and what has kept him so long and why was it that he wasn't in the area just before the machine broke down. Make sure you give the impression that you firmly believe that YOUR machine has absolute priority over everyone else - what the hell are you paying for anyway? Before he has a chance to wipe off the looks of amazement, ask him how soon the machine will be operational. If he looks devastated by this mention that you are about to phone the service manager and complain about his lack of communication and technical competence.

4 Always have some of the aforementioned people on hand to interrupt him and ask technical questions, preferably ones that are in no way directly connected with actually operating the machine.

5 Don't forget to frequently interrupt the people that are interrupting him to ask how long repairs will take - keep mentioning the service manager.

6 If possible, without inconveniencing yourself, arrange to call for service late, say at 5.00 p.m. FRIDAY IS A GOOD DAY; you can insist on completion by 9.00 a.m. Monday.

7 Periodically (during the interruptions) tell the engineer what excellent service you get from other organisations.

8 When he does eventually finish make it clear that it took too long.

9 When he leaves phone up his office and tell them the machine is worse than ever and won't do. This will force the service engineer to return and gives you a chance to put him through the whole thing again.

TROUBLESHOOTING FLOWCHART

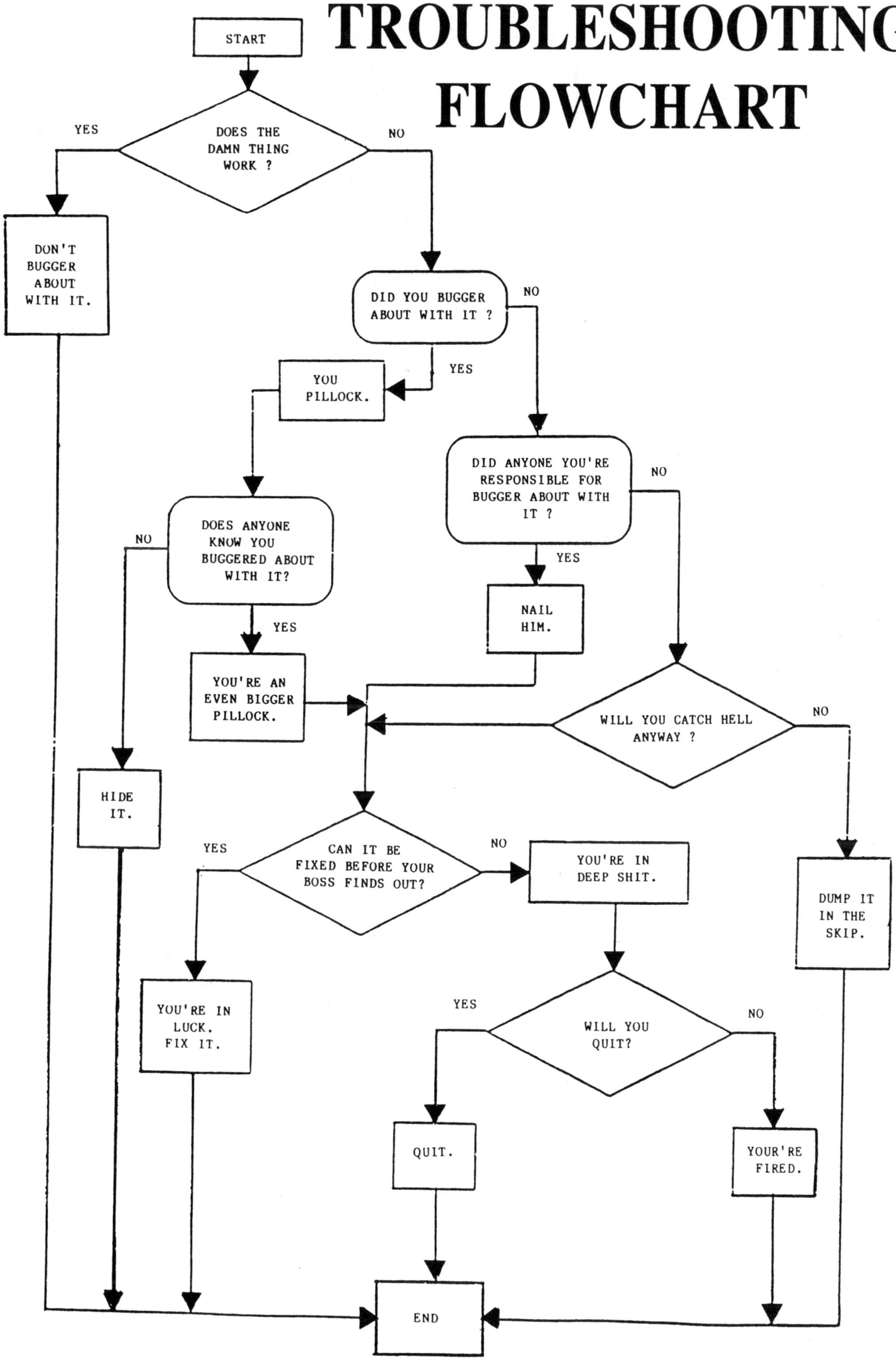
START
DOES THE DAMN THING WORK ?
YES
NO
DON'T BUGGER ABOUT WITH IT.
DID YOU BUGGER ABOUT WITH IT ?
NO
YES
YOU PILLOCK.
DID ANYONE YOU'RE RESPONSIBLE FOR BUGGER ABOUT WITH IT ?
NO
YES
DOES ANYONE KNOW YOU BUGGERED ABOUT WITH IT?
NO
YES
NAIL HIM.
YOU'RE AN EVEN BIGGER PILLOCK.
WILL YOU CATCH HELL ANYWAY ?
NO
HIDE IT.
CAN IT BE FIXED BEFORE YOUR BOSS FINDS OUT?
YES
NO
YOU'RE IN DEEP SHIT.
DUMP IT IN THE SKIP.
YOU'RE IN LUCK. FIX IT.
WILL YOU QUIT?
YES
NO
QUIT.
YOUR'RE FIRED.
END

'LET ME GET THIS STRAIGHT, MY COMPLAINT WAS RELAYED FROM YOUR NIGHT ANSWERING MACHINE TO A COMPUTER WHICH THEN PRINTED OUT MY DATA ON TAPE WHICH WAS THEN TRANSFERRED TO A READER WHICH CORRELATED ALL COMPLAINTS BY AREA AND TYPE, AND THEN - THE CARRIER PIGEON BECAME ILL"?!

GENERAL GOODS CORPORATION

An American company sent a shipment of rice to an account in Hamburg, Germany.

En route, mice chewed holes in the bags, nested in the rice and damaged the shipment. The shipping concern, however, sewed up the bags and sent them to the destination. Two weeks late, the American company received the following letter from their account:

Hans Grubeck
Jungfernstem 36
Hamburg
Germany

General Goods Corporation
Green Rice Purchasing Dept
Cotton Exchange Building
New York, N.Y.

Shentlemane,
Der last schipment of rice ve got from you vas with mice schidt gomixt. Der rice vas gut enhoff, but der schidt schpoiled der trade. Ve did not see der mice schidt in der sample you sent us.

It takes too much time to pick der mice schidt durts out from der rice. Ve order kleen rice und you schipt schidt. It vas a mistake, yes, no?

Ve like you to schip us der rice in vun sack und der mice schidt in annudder sack, und den ve gomix to soot der customer. Please write if ve should schip back der schidt und keep der rice, or schip der rice und keep der schidt, or schip back der hole schitten verkes.

Ve vant to do vat is rite in diss matter, ve do not like diss mice schidt business.

Mitt much respeckt.

(signed) Hans Grubeck
Pee Ass: Is der price der same mitt or mittout?

COMMUNICATION

1. Read everything before you do anything.

2. Put your name in the upper right-hand corner of the paper, in the space provided.

3. Circle the word "name" in the second sentence, above.

4. Draw five small squares in the upper left-hand corner of this paper.

5. Put an X in each of the five small squares you have drawn.

6. Put a circle around each of those five small squares above.

7. Sign your name, under and to the left of the title above.

8. Draw a circle, in pen, around sentences 6 and 7 above.

9. Multiply 70 x 30 and write the result on the reverse side.

10. Draw a circle around the word "paper" in sentence 4, above.

11. Please now call out your first name, loudly.

12. If you feel that you have carefully followed these directions, call out, loudly: I have carefully followed directions!"

13. Add 107 and 278, and write the sum on the reverse, immediately under the first figure that you wrote there.

14. Circle that figure on the reverse.

15. In a normal voice, count aloud from 1 - 10.

16. If no one else has said it, say now, "I am the leader!".

17. Now that you have read all of the foregoing, very carefully, please complete ONLY sentences 1 and 2.

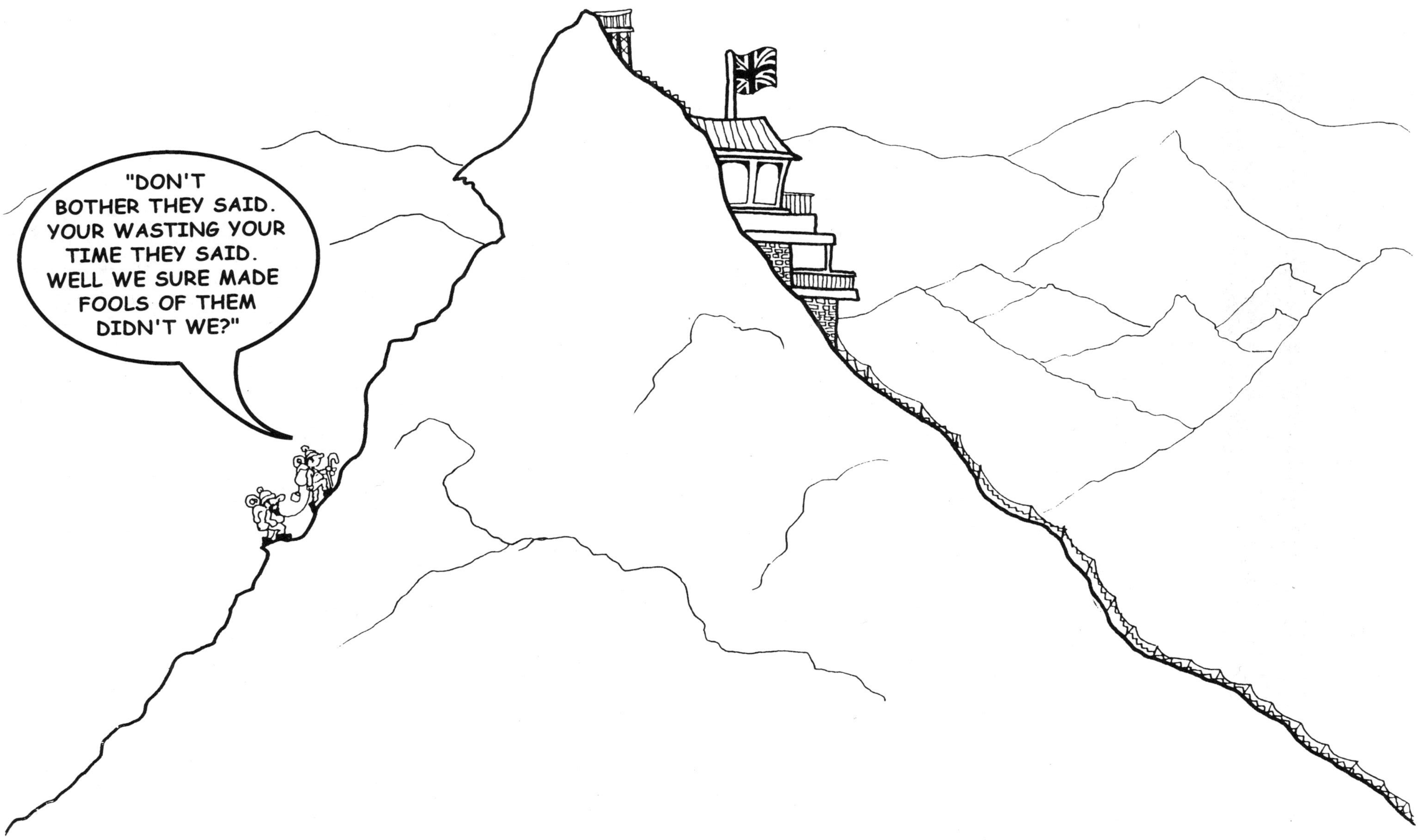
"DON'T BOTHER THEY SAID. YOUR WASTING YOUR TIME THEY SAID. WELL WE SURE MADE FOOLS OF THEM DIDN'T WE?"

I'm fine thank you

There is nothing the matter with me,
I'm as healthy as I can be.
I have arthritis in both my knees
And when I talk, I talk with a wheeze.
My pulse is weak, and my blood is thin,
But I'm awfully well for the shape I'm in.

Arch supports I have for my feet,
Or I wouldn't be able to be on the street.
Sleep is denied me night after night.
But every morning I find I'm alright.
My memory is failing, my head's in a spin
But I'm awfully well for the shape I'm in.

How do I know that my youth is all spent?
Well my "Get up and go" has got up and went.
But I really don't mind when I think with a grin,
Of all the grand places my "Get up" has bin.

Old age is golden I've heard it said
But, sometimes I wonder as I get into bed.
With my ears in the drawer, my teeth in a cup,
My eyes on the table until I wake up.
Ere sleep overtakes me, I say to myself,
Is there anything else I could lay on the shelf?"

I get up each morning and dust off my wits
And pick up the paper and read the "Obits"
If my name is still missing I know I'm not dead,
So I have a good breakfast and go back to bed.

HOW TO KNOW
YOU ARE GROWING OLDER

Everything hurts and what doesn't hurt, doesn't work.

The gleam in your eye is from the sun hitting your bifocals.

You feel like the night before, and you haven't been anywhere.

Your little black book contains only the names ending in M.D.

Your mind makes commitments your body can't meet.

You know all the answers, but nobody asks you the questions.

You walk with your head held high trying to get used to your bifocals.

You turn out the light for economic rather than romantic reasons.

You sit in the rocking chair and can't get it going.

You're startled the first time you are addressed as old-timer.

You get winded playing chess.

Your children begin to look middle aged.

You join a health club and don't go.

You begin to outlive enthusiasm.

You look forward to a dull evening.

You sit in the rocking chair and can't get it going.

Your knees buckle and your belt won't.

You regret all those mistakes resisting temptation.

You stop looking forward to your next birthday.

Dialling long distance wears you out.

You remember today, that yesterday was your Wedding Anniversary.

You finally reach the top of the ladder and find it leaning against the wrong wall.

You're 17 around the neck, 42 around the waist, and 108 round the golf course.

"BOY! WAS I DRUNK LAST NIGHT! I DON'T EVEN REMEMBER YOUR NAME!"

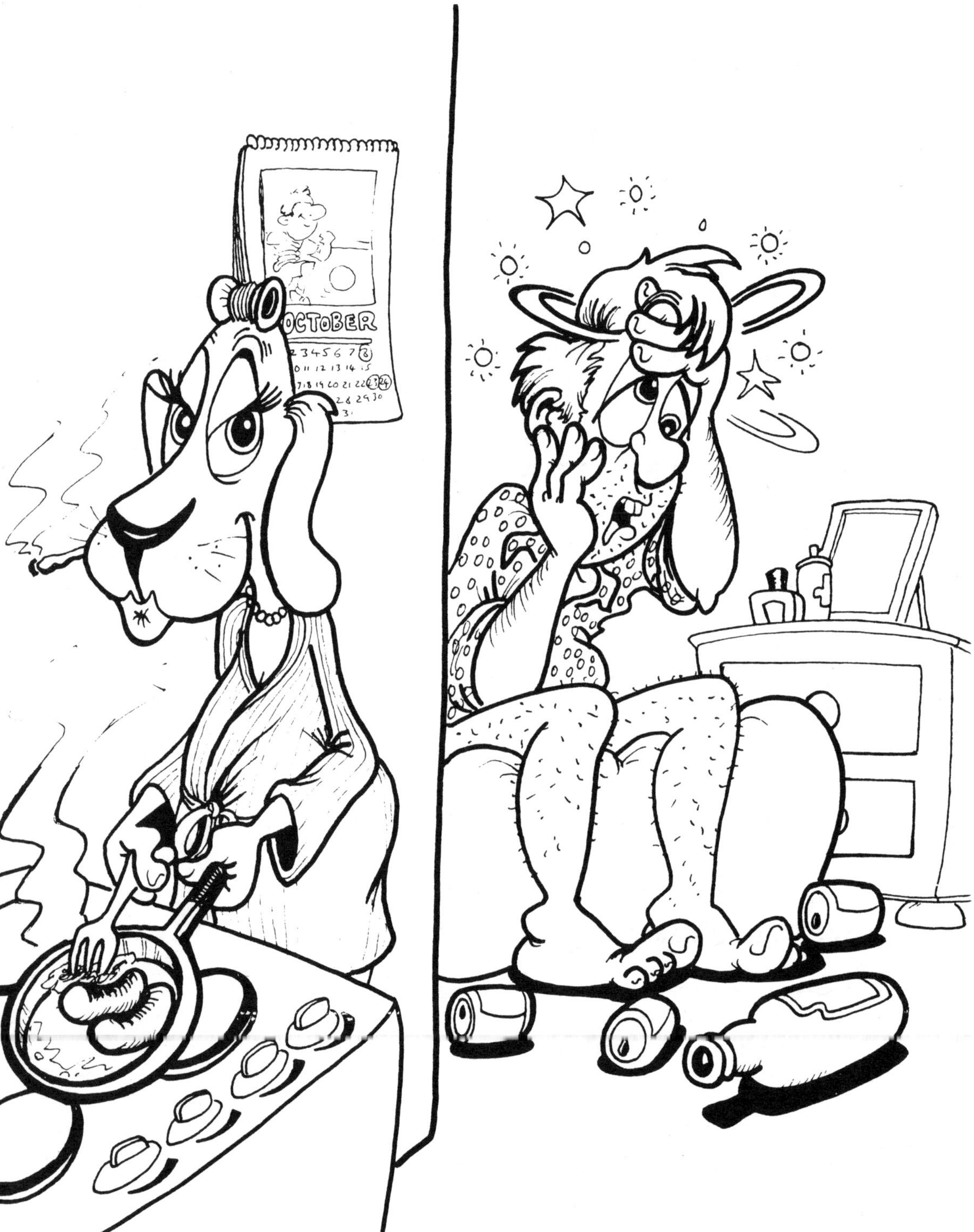
OCTOBER

MEN BASHING

1 **WHAT DO YOU CALL A MAN WITH AN IQ OF 50?**
Gifted.

2 **HOW CAN YOU TELL IF A MAN IS HAPPY?**
Who cares.

3 **WHAT DO MEN AN BEER BOTTLES HAVE IN COMMON?**
They're both empty from the neck up.

4 **HOW MANY MEN DOES IT TAKE TO CHANGE A ROLL OF TOILET PAPER?**
We don't know, it's never happened.

5 **WHY DO MEN ALWAYS HAVE STUPID LOOKS ON THEIR?**
Because they are stupid.

6 **WHY ARE BLONDE JOKES SO SHORT?**
So men can remember them.

7 **WHAT IS THE THINNEST BOOK IN THE WORLD?**
What men know about women.

8 **HOW DO YOU SAVE A MAN FROM DROWNING?**
Take your foot off his head.

THE REV HAROLD KNIGHT.
THE RESCUE MISSION.
195 ELLIOT ROAD, CAMBERWELL GREEN,
CAMBERWELL. LONDON. W1C

Dear

Perhaps you have heard of me and my nationwide campaign, in the cause of temperance. Each year for the past fourteen, I have made a tour of Scotland, England and Wales, and have delivered a series of lectures on the evils of drinking and drugs. On this tour I have been accompanied by a young friend and assistant, by the name of Joseph Powell. Joe a young man of good family and excellent background, is a pathetic example of a life ruined by excessive indulgence in whisky, pot and women.

Joe would appear with me at the lecture and sit on the platform, wheezing and staring at the audience through bleary, bloodshot eyes, sweating profusely, picking his nose, passing wind and making obscene gestures, while I would point him out as an example of what drinking etc. can do to a person.

Last summer, unfortunately, Joe died. A mutual friend has given me your name and address and I wonder if you would care to take Joe's place on my next tour?

Yours in the faith,

Rev Harold Knight
Rescue Mission.

Believe it or not, the following announcements actually appeared in various church bulletins.

1 Don't let worry kill you - let the church help.

2 Thursday night - Potluck supper. Prayer and medication to follow.

3 Remember in prayer the many who are sick of our church and community.

4 For those of you who have children and don't know it, we have a nursery downstairs.

5 This afternoon there will be a meeting in the South and North ends of the church. Children will be baptised at both ends.

6 Tuesday at 4:00 PM there will be an ice cream social. All ladies giving milk will please come early.

7 This being Easter Sunday, we will ask Mrs. Lewis to come forward and lay an egg on the alter.

8 The service will close with "Little Drops of Water." One of the ladies will start quietly and the rest of the congregation will join in.

9 Next Sunday a special collection will be taken to defray the cost of the new carpet. All those wishing to do something on the new carpet will come forward and do so.

"WELL GENTLEMEN, LET ME WELCOME YOU TO A RATHER EARLY START FOR THE FIFTH DAY OF THIS, THE FIRST INTERNATIONAL SEMINAR ON SLEEP PSYCHOLOGY...."

I'm Tired

Yes I'm tired. For several years I've been blaming it on middle age, poor blood, lack of vitamins, air pollution, saccharin, obesity, dieting, under arm odour, yellow wax build up and another dozen maladies that make you wonder if life is worth living.

But I find out it isn't that.

I'm tired because I'm overworked.

The population of this country is 51 million and 21 million are retired. That leaves 30 million to do the work. There are 19 million in school. That leaves 11 million. Of this total 2 million are unemployed and 4 million are employed by the government. That leaves 5 million to do the work. One million are in the armed forces which leaves 4 million to do the work. From that total, 3 million are employed by County and Borough Councils, leaving 1 million people to do the work. There are 62,000 people in hospital and 937,998 people in prisons.

That leaves 2 people to do the work.

You and me.

And you are sitting on your arse reading this.

No wonder I'm bloody tired.

THERE IS ONLY TWO THINGS IN THIS WORLD.................

There is only two things in this world to worry about,

Are you going to be rich?

Or are you going to be poor?

If you are going to be rich you won't have anything to worry about.

If you are going to be poor, you only have two things to worry about.

Are you going to be healthy?

Or are you going to be sick?

If you are going to be healthy, you have nothing to worry about.

If you are going to be sick, you only have two things to worry about,

Are you going to live?

Or are you going to die?

If you live you have nothing to worry about.

If you die you will have two things to worry about.

Are you going to go up?

Or are you going to go down?

If you go up you have nothing to worry about.

If you go down, you will have nothing to worry about,

Because all your friends will be there to meet you.

"STRESS"

THE CONFUSION CREATED WHEN ONE'S MIND OVERRIDES THE BODY'S BASIC DESIRE TO CHOKE THE LIVING DAYLIGHTS OUT OF SOMEONE WHO DESPERATELY NEEDS IT!

If you can keep your head when all those about you are losing their's - YOU'RE NOT AWARE OF THE SITUATION!

IF YOU WANT MATTERS TO STAY AS THEY ARE, THINGS ARE GOING TO HAVE TO CHANGE!

ALWAYS INSIST THAT WHERE YOU ARE IS WHERE YOU WERE GOING - BECAUSE NO MATTER WHERE YOU GO, THERE YOU ARE!

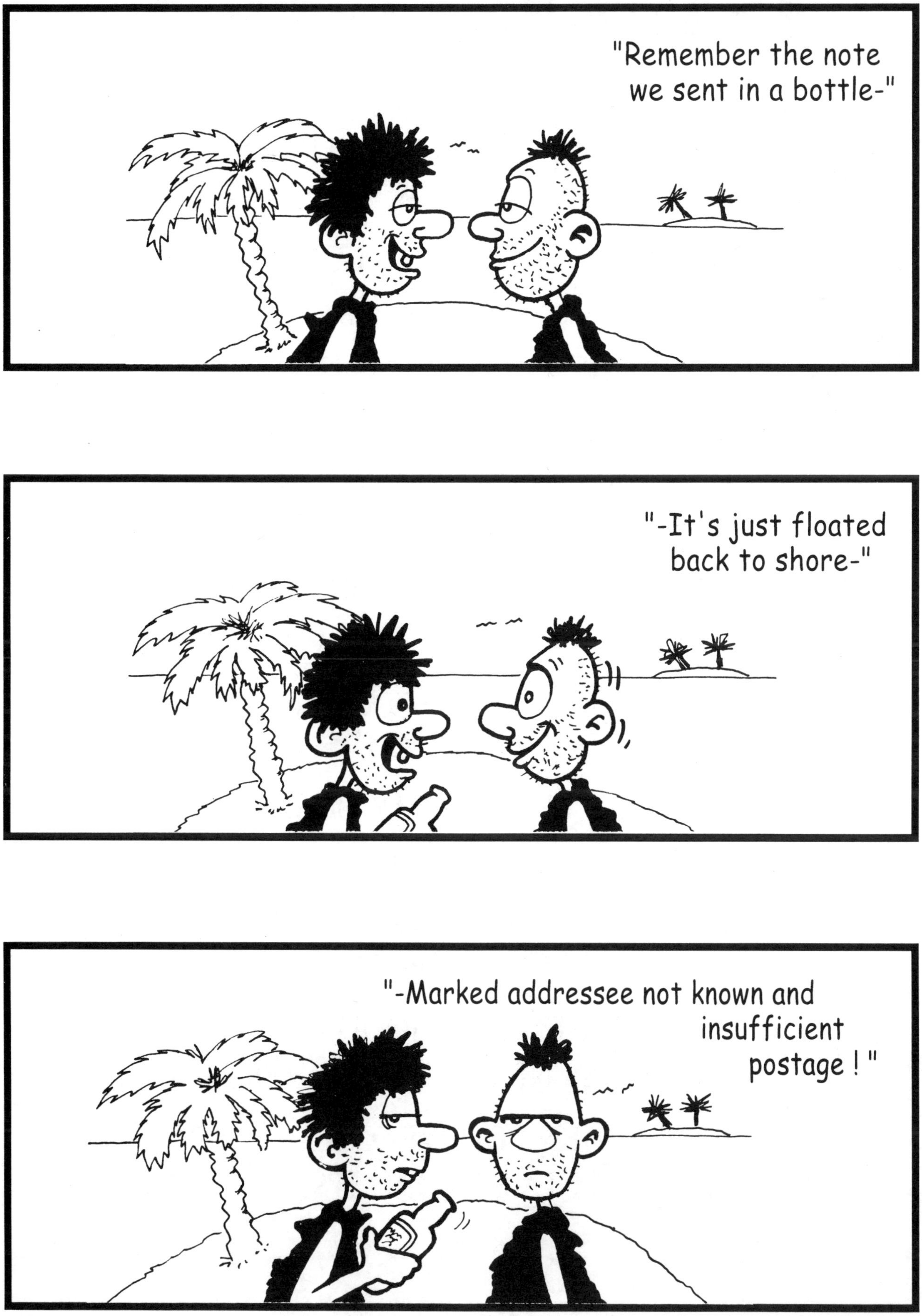
"Remember the note we sent in a bottle-"
"-It's just floated back to shore-"
"-Marked addressee not known and insufficient postage ! "

MATTER OF INTERPRETATION

WHEN I TAKE A LONG TIME -
I'M SLOW.

WHEN MY BOSS TAKES A LONG TIME -
HE'S THOROUGH.

WHEN I DON'T DO IT -
I'M LAZY.

WHEN MY BOSS DOESN'T DO IT -
HE IS TOO BUSY.

WHEN I DO SOMETHING WITHOUT BEING TOLD -
I AM TRYING TO BE SMART.

WHEN MY BOSS DOES THE SAME -
THAT'S INITIATIVE.

WHEN I PLEASE MY BOSS -
THAT IS CREEPING.

WHEN MY BOSS PLEASES HIS BOSS -
HE'S CO-OPERATING.

WHEN I DO GOOD -
MY BOSS NEVER REMEMBERS

WHEN I DO WRONG -
HE NEVER FORGETS!

THE EVOLUTION OF AUTHORITY

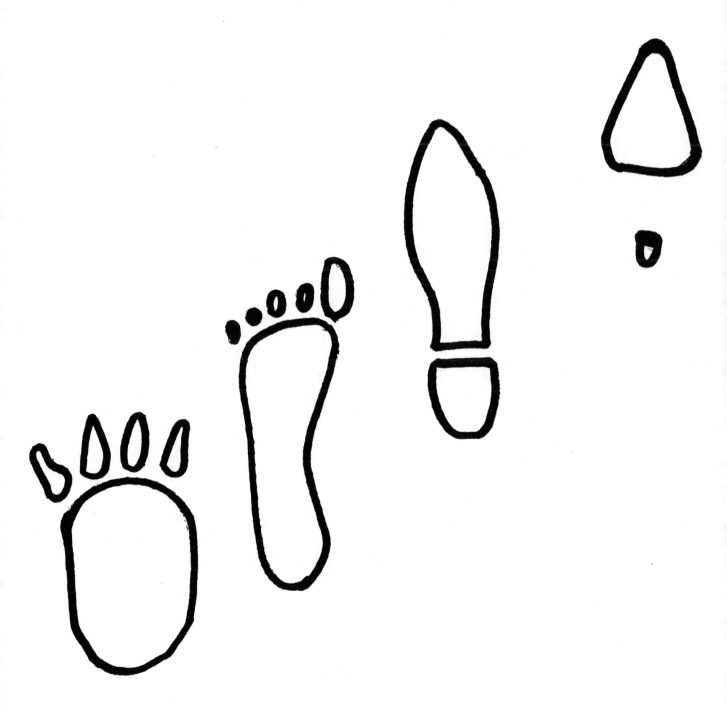

So You Want The Day Off

Let's take a look at what your asking.

There are 365 days per year available for work.
There are 52 weeks per year in which you already
have two days off per week leaving 261 days
available for work.
Since you spend 19 hours each day away from work,
you have used up 170 days, leaving only 91 days
available.
You spend 30 minutes each day on coffee breaks,
that accounts for 23 days each year, leaving only 68
days available.
With one hour lunch period each day, you have used
up another 46 days, leaving only 22 days available
for work.
You normally spend 2 days on sick leave, this leaves
only 20 days available for work.
We are off 5 holidays per year, so your available
working time is down to 15 days.
We generously give you 14 days vacation per year
which leaves only 1 day available for work and I'll
be damned if you're going to take that day OFF!!

ABSENTEEISM

As stated in a previous notice, there has been an alarming increase in absenteeism. The planned address on this subject by the Managing Director has been postponed since he is away at the moment.

SPECIFIC ORGANISATIONAL OPTIONS - BEING LIMITED, AND GIVEN CURRENT RESTRICTIONS IN PERFORMANCE MODES WE SEE SEVERE RESTRAINTS ON THE CHOICES AND PROBABILITIES LIKELY TO CHARACTERISE RE-ENGAGEMENT OF YOUR SERVICES - IN SHORT, YOU'RE FIRED!

REASONS WHY A COMPUTER MUST BE FEMALE

1. No one but their creator understands their internal logic.

2. Even your smallest mistakes are immediately committed to memory for future reference.

3. The native language used to communicate with other computers is incomprehensible to everyone else.

4. The message "Bad command or file name" is about as informative as "If you don't know why I'm mad at you, I'm certainly not going to tell you."

5. As soon as you make a commitment to one, you find yourself spending half your paycheck on accessories for it.

WIFE 1.0

Last year a friend upgraded from Girlfriend 1.0 to Wife 1.0 and found that it's a memory hog leaving very little system resources for other applications. He is only now noticing that Wife 1.0 also is spawning Child-Processes which are further consuming valuable system resources. No mention of this particular phenomena was included in the product brochure or the documentation, though other users have informed him that this is to be expected due to the nature of the application.

Not only that Wife 1.0 installs itself such that it is always launched at system initialisation where it can monitor all other system activity. He's finding that some applications like PokerNight 10.0, BeerBash 2.5, and PubNight 7.0 are no longer able to run on the system at all, crashing the system when selected (even though they always worked fine before).

At installation, Wife 1.0 provides no option as to the installation of undesired Plug-Ins such as Mother-In-Law 55.8 and Brother-In-Law Beta release. Also, system performance seams to diminish with each passing day. The features he would like to see in the upcoming Wife-2.0 include:

- A "Don't remind me again" button.
- Minimise button.
- An install shield feature that allows Wife 2.0 to be installed with the option to uninstall at any time without the loss of cache and other system resources.
- An option to run the network driver in promiscuous mode which would allow the system hardware probe feature to be much more useful.

I myself decided to avoid the headaches associated with Wife 1.0 by sticking with Girlfriend 2.0 Even here, however, I found many problems. Apparently you cannot install Girlfriend 2.0 on top of Girlfriend 1.0. You have to completely uninstall Girlfriend 1.0 first.
To make matters worse, the uninstall program for Girlfriend 1.0 doesn't work very well leaving undesirable traces of the application in the system. Another thing sucks - all versions of Girlfrined continually pop-up little messages about upgrading to Wife 1.0.

BUG WARNING

Wife 1.0 has an undocumented bug. If you try to install Mistress 1.1 before uninstalling Wife 1.0, Wife 1.0 will delete MSMoney files before claiming insufficient resources.

JUST BECAUSE YOUR PARANOID DOESN'T MEAN THEY AREN'T OUT TO GET YOU.

IF YOU HAVE BLUNDERED,
AND YOU'RE FEELING TWO INCHES TALL,
SEEING A GLOATING FACE LOOKING FROM
EVERY CORNER,
TAKE HEART,
NO ONE REMEMBERS THE TITANIC'S CAPTAIN,
SO WHAT MAKES YOUR BOO-BOO
MEMORABLE?

(Yes they do, his name was Captain E.J.Smith!)

ALMOST ANYTHING IS EASIER TO GET INTO THAN OUT OF.

PASSING WIND DO'S and DONT'S

An invaluable guide to passing wind at Royal and Diplomatic Garden parties, receptions and investitures

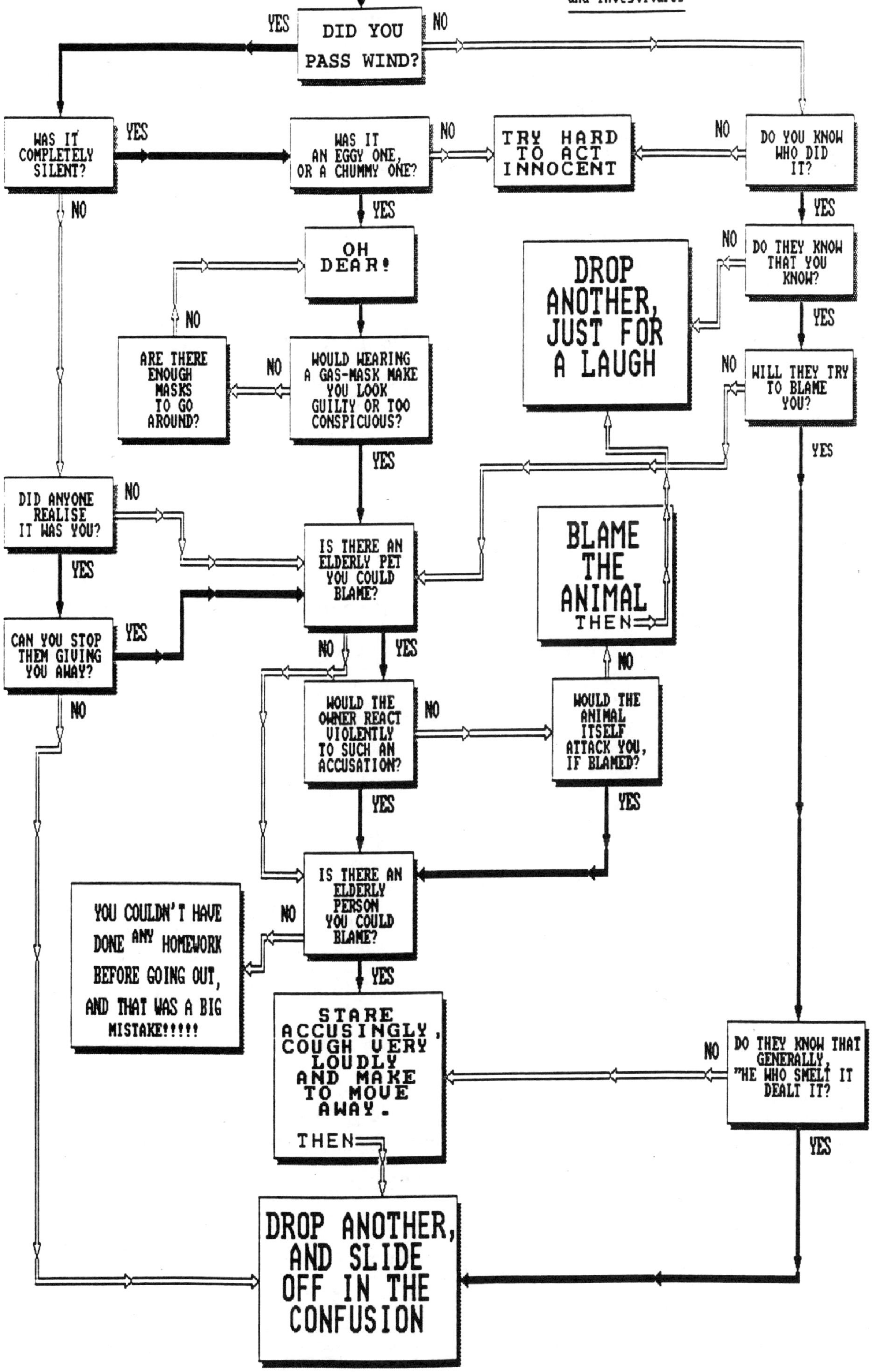
DID YOU PASS WIND?
WAS IT COMPLETELY SILENT?
WAS IT AN EGGY ONE, OR A CHUMMY ONE?
TRY HARD TO ACT INNOCENT
DO YOU KNOW WHO DID IT?
OH DEAR!
DO THEY KNOW THAT YOU KNOW?
DROP ANOTHER, JUST FOR A LAUGH
ARE THERE ENOUGH MASKS TO GO AROUND?
WOULD WEARING A GAS-MASK MAKE YOU LOOK GUILTY OR TOO CONSPICUOUS?
WILL THEY TRY TO BLAME YOU?
DID ANYONE REALISE IT WAS YOU?
IS THERE AN ELDERLY PET YOU COULD BLAME?
BLAME THE ANIMAL THEN
CAN YOU STOP THEM GIVING YOU AWAY?
WOULD THE OWNER REACT VIOLENTLY TO SUCH AN ACCUSATION?
WOULD THE ANIMAL ITSELF ATTACK YOU, IF BLAMED?
IS THERE AN ELDERLY PERSON YOU COULD BLAME?
YOU COULDN'T HAVE DONE ANY HOMEWORK BEFORE GOING OUT, AND THAT WAS A BIG MISTAKE!!!!!
STARE ACCUSINGLY, COUGH VERY LOUDLY AND MAKE TO MOVE AWAY. THEN
DO THEY KNOW THAT GENERALLY, "HE WHO SMELT IT DEALT IT?
DROP ANOTHER, AND SLIDE OFF IN THE CONFUSION
YES
NO

Once upon a time, U.K. plc and the Japanese decided to have a boat race on the River Thames. Both teams practiced long and hard to reach their peak performance. On the big day, they were as ready as they could be. The Japanese won by a mile.

Afterwards, the U.K. plc team became very discouraged and moral sagged. Senior Management decoded that the reason for the crushing defeat had to be found, and a project team was set up in the New Forest to investigate the problem and recommend action. Their conclusion: the problem was that the Japanese team had eight people rowing and one person steering. The U.K. plc team had one person rowing and eight people steering.

Senior management immediately hired a consultancy company to carry out a study on the team's structure. Millions of pounds and several months later they concluded that: too many people were steering and too few were rowing.

Aiming to win the next race, the team structure was changed to four 'steering managers', three 'senior steering managers' and one 'executive steering manager'. A performance and appraisal system was set up to give the person rowing the boat more incentive to work harder and become a key performer. "We must give him empowerment and enrichment. This ought to do it"!

At the end of the next race the Japanese had won by two moles. U.K. plc laid off the rower for poor performance, sold off all the paddles, cancelled all capital investment for new equipment, halted development of a new canoe, awarded high performance awards to the consultants and distributed the remaining money saved to senior management.

ORGANISATIONAL CHART

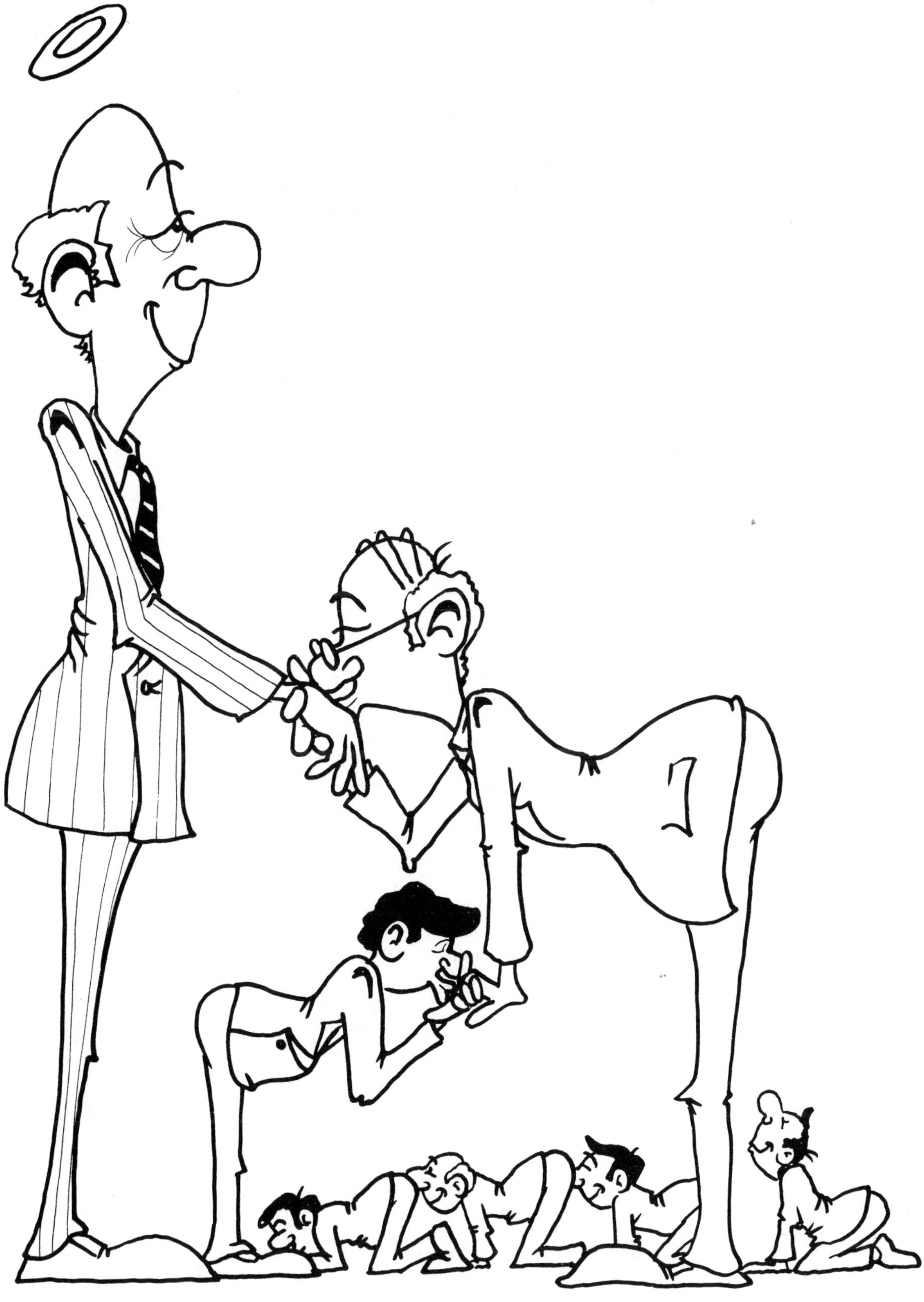

LOO-DILEMMA

No.9 in the Series:

a Flowcharting Guide to Life

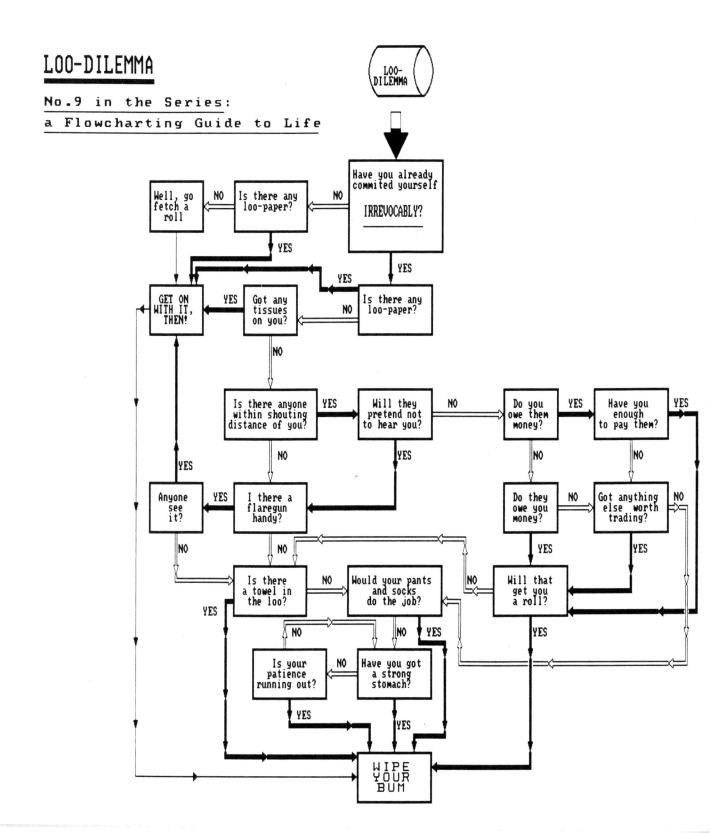

TO ALL STAFF
SUBJECT: TAX RETURNS

You can book now for a series of three one-hour lectures on how to avoid a coronary when called to the Inland Revenue to explain your tax return. In the first session, topics include: spontaneous weeping, lip - biting till it bleeds, hand - wringing, sucking sweat droplets off your nose and incessant snuffling. Various sources for blood pellets (simulating internal haemorrhaging)
and false limbs (dramatically tossed at the I.R. man with the cry "Don't hurt me, I'm a leper") are given.

The second lecture describes various body pressure points so, as you pretend to light your umpteenth cigarette, you can cause self-induced and instantaneous loss of consciousness (abruptly interrupting the I.R. mans stream of obscenities and making it impossible to answer his demands that you prove your 9 dependents and claim for less than 90 days U.K. residency).
Various pain killers are described, guaranteed to suppress a confession when the rubber hoses come out.

Lecture three details faking documentary evidence for the 11 kids you claim to support and methods of successfully falsifying bank statements, as does the penultimate section which covers methods of proving you were insane or suffering from the plague at the time of filling in your return.
A complete list of all I.R personnel in your tax district is available including a comprehensive survey of all the unsavoury aspects of their personal lives (under the title 'A Little Blackmail can Soften the Blow')

Diplomacy is to do and say
the nastiest things in the nicest way.

I'm sure you understand what it is you think I said, but I'm not sure you realise that what I said was not what I meant.

I intended to make it clear that what I mean to say cannot be misunderstood, and that any misunderstanding is the fault of your own believing that your interpretation of what you thought I said is infallible.

As you decrease the length of an argument, you increase it's impact, and the more impact it has the more likely you are to get into an argument.

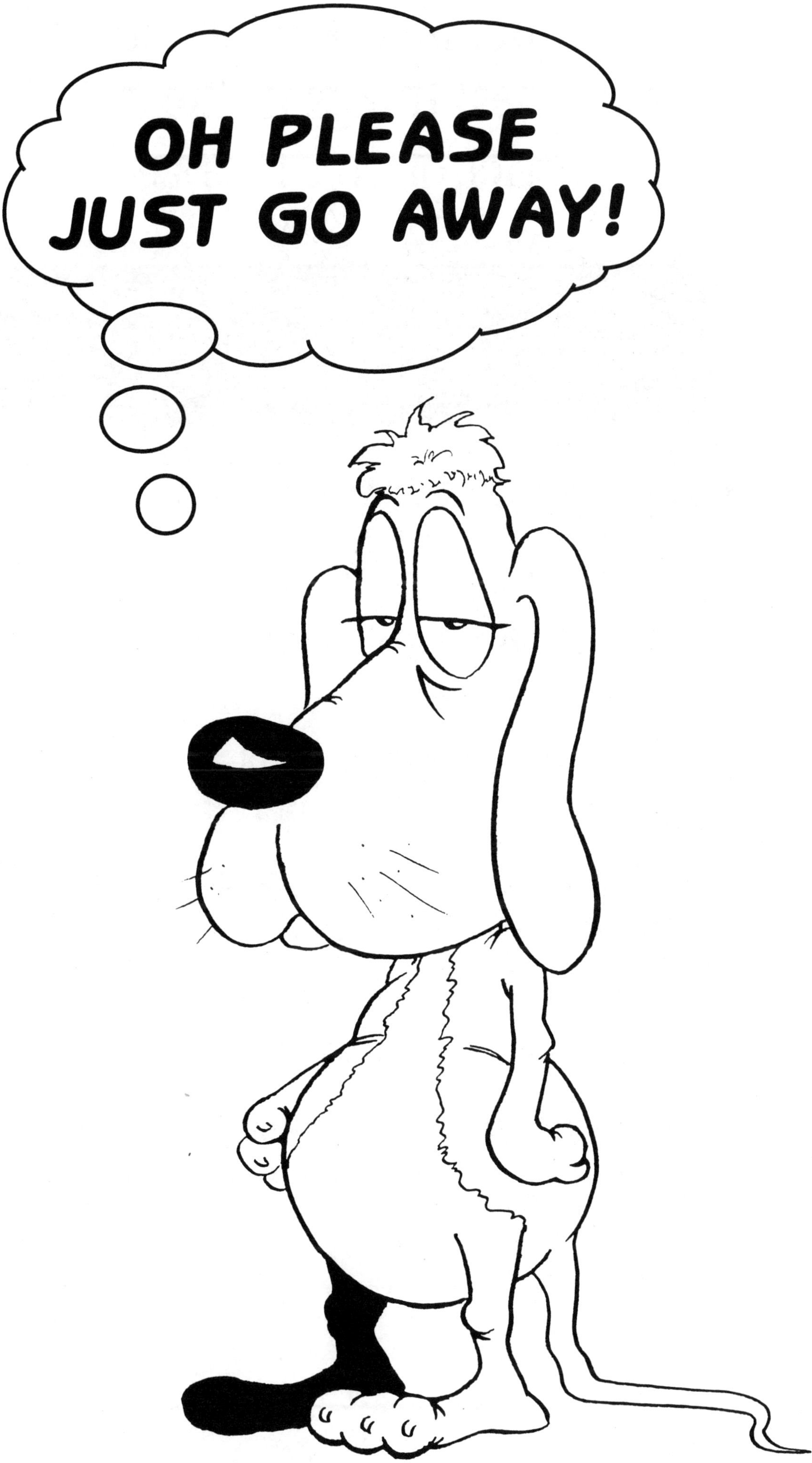
OH PLEASE JUST GO AWAY!

NOTICE

OFFICE OF CIVILIAN DEFENCE
WASHINGTON, D.C.

INSTRUCTIONS TO PATRONS ON PREMISES IN CASE OF NUCLEAR BOMB ATTACK:

UPON THE FIRST WARNING:

1. Stay clear of all windows.

2. Keep hands free of glasses, bottles, cigarettes, etc.

3. Stand away from bar, tables, orchestra, equipment and furniture.

4. Loosen necktie, unbutton coat and any other restrictive clothing.

5. Remove glasses, empty pockets of all sharp objects such as pens, pencils, etc.

6. Immediately upon seeing the brilliant flash of nuclear explosion, bend over and place your head firmly between your legs.

7. Then kiss your ass goodbye.

"PHILOSOPHER'S CORNER"

SOCIALISM.
*You have two cows
and give one to your neighbour.*

COMMUNISM
*You have two cows;
the government takes both and gives you the milk.*

FASCISM
*You have two cows;
the government takes both and sells you the milk.*

NAZISM
*You have two cows;
the government takes both and shoots you.*

BUREAUCRATISM
*You have two cows;
the government takes both, shoots one,
milks the other and throws the milk away.*

CAPITALISM
*You have two cows;
you sell one and buy a bull.*

FUNCTIONS OF THE EXECUTIVE

As nearly everyone knows, the executive has practically nothing to do except to decide what is to be done; to tell somebody to do it; to listen why it should not be done, why it should be done by somebody else, or why it should be done in a different way. To follow up to see if the thing has been done; to discover that it has not; to enquire why: to listen to excuses from the person who should have done it; to follow it up again and to see if the thing has been done, only to discover that it has been done incorrectly; to point out how it should have been done; to conclude that as long as it has been done, it may as well be left as it is.

To wonder if it is not the time to get rid of a person who cannot do a thing right; to reflect that he probably has a wife and a large family and that certainly any successor would be just as bad, and maybe worse. To consider how much simpler and better the things would have been if one had done it oneself in the first place, to reflect sadly that one could have done it right in 20 minutes and, as things turned out, one has to spend two days to find out why it has taken three weeks for somebody else to do it wrong.

'I'M SORRY SMITH, BUT BEING ABLE TO SKATE AROUND ALL NINE OF THE COMPANIES DEPARTMENTS COMPLETELY BLINDFOLDED DOES QUALIFY YOU FOR SENIOR MANAGEMENT"!

A SHORT HISTORY OF MEDICINE

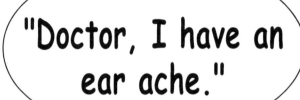

"Doctor, I have an ear ache."

2000 BC. "Here, eat this root."

1000 BC. "That root is heathen, say this prayer."

1000 AD. "That prayer is heathen - pray to Christ."

1850 AD. "That prayer is superstition - drink this potion."

1940 AD. "That potion is snake oil - take this pill."

1985 AD. "That pill is ineffective - take this antibiotic"

2000 AD. "That antibiotic is artificial - here eat this root."

NOTICE

MOST EMPLOYEES WILL KNOW THAT OUR PRESENT FACTORY PREMISES GO BACK TO THE 1850'S. RECENT EXTENSION WORK TO THE PLATING SHOP REVEALED AN ALMOST PERFECTLY PRESERVED MACHINE SHOP OF EARLY VINTAGE. A MUMMIFIED WORKER OF THE PERIOD WAS FOUND SLUMPED OVER ONE OF THE MACHINES – APPARENTLY HE DIED OF EXHAUSTION AND THE INHUMAN CONDITIONS PREVAILING AT THE TIME.

VISITS TO THE AREA WILL NOT BE APPROVED – MANAGEMENT BELIEVE STAFF MAY BECOME ENVIOUS AND DISCONTENT WITH THE CURRENT WORKING ENVIRONMENT.

NOTE TO PROSPECTIVE APPLICANTS IN SALES

Those of you scanning the Press for a job in Sales and Marketing had best beware of the applied psychology and sheet dishonesty of some companies. A good marker of what you can expect is given in the phraseology used in their Ads for recruiting sales staff:

1. **'YOUNG DYNAMIC CO.'** – A one man band – he'll be the conductor and you'll play all the instruments.

2. **'SALARY RELATED TO EFFORT'** – Commission only – can you afford it?

3. **'SKY'S THE LIMIT'** – They'll hustle for a sky-high sales target and push you to your limit!

4. **'RAPID PROMOTION'** – Drop-out rate of sales staff is so high that if you survive a week or two you become eligible for the company's debts.

5. **'VIGOROUS AND DEDICATED APPLICANTS BELOW 25 ONLY'** – Low salary and commission – cold calling through the night on trainees' income.

6. **'NO EXPERIENCE NECESSARY'** – Works on probability that out of the 3 or 4 hundred guys they hire (and fire) each week one of them should make a sale.

7. **'PROFESSIONAL WITH PROVEN TRACK RECORD'** – They're poaching – out of the many applicants one will probably have the contacts they want. If you've been selling cars, and they're into paint, forget it!

8. **'FIVE YEARS AGO I WAS PENNILESS – LET ME SHOW YOU HOW TO MAKE £50,000 A YEAR'** – He can't be bright so he must be dishonest. How else do you go from poverty to riches by showing someone else how to become poor?

9. **'MARKET LEADERS – UNIQUE PRODUCT'** – Naturally, who else sells orange flavoured washing-up liquid.

10. **'ALL LEADS SUPPLIED'** – You're cold calling in dog foods and the leads are free gifts.

11. **'CHALLENGING POSITION FOR DEDICATED SALES EXECUTIVE'** – They're operating in a highly competitive market and losing ground – if you are a sales equivalent to a Sherman tank, ruthless, unscrupulous and love to be hated – this could be for you.

FIBBER ADVERTISING AGENCY

GUIDELINES FOR ADVERTISERS

1, The truth is what you make it,

   so

2, Don't tell lies when you can use statistics.

3, The World is golden unless seen through rose coloured spectacles.

4, The manufacturer has no part in saying what his product can do.

5, Sincerity sells, once you can fake it you can't lose.

6, You can fool 88.75% of the public all the time, the rest haven't got any money.

7, If the product fits into the actresses cleavage, she's not big enough for the job.

8, If the product kills 10% of the market, that still leaves you the remaining 100%.

9, If the product sells, it's due to good advertising exposure, if it doesn't, it's due to bad product design.

EVERY DAY OF MY LIFE I'M FORCED TO ADD ANOTHER NAME TO THE LIST OF PEOPLE WHO REALLY GET ON MY NERVES

PERMANENT LIST

_____
_____
_____
_____
_____
_____
_____
_____
_____
_____
_____
_____
_____
_____

LIST FOR TODAY

_____
_____
_____
_____
_____
_____
_____
_____
_____
_____
_____
_____
_____

A SHORT COURSE IN HUMAN RELATIONS

SIX MOST IMPORTANT WORDS-
"I ADMIT I MADE A MISTAKE"

FIVE MOST IMPORTANT WORDS -
"YOU DID A GOOD JOB".

FOUR MOST IMPORTANT WORDS -
"WHAT IS YOUR OPINION "?

THREE MOST IMPORTANT WORDS -
"IF YOU PLEASE -"

TWO MOST IMPORTANT WORDS -
"THANK YOU -"

ONE MOST IMPORTANT WORD -
"WE -".

ONE LEAST IMPORTANT WORD -
"I".

IF ALL THIS FAILS, REMEMBER THE PARAMOUNT
PHRASE - **"GO STEW YOUR HEAD FISHFACE"!**

A Glossary of Business Terms!

A Consultant - Anyone with a briefcase more than 25 miles form home.

An Expert - Someone who avoids all the small errors as they sweep towards the ultimate mistake.

A Colleague - Someone called in at the last minute to share the blame.

A Reliable Source - Someone you just met.

An Informed Source - The person who told the person you just met.

An Unimpeachable Source - The person who started the rumour in the first place.

A Meeting - A mass mulling of master minds.

A Conference - A place where conversation relieves the dreariness of work and the loneliness of thought.

A Programme - Anything that can't be covered by one 'phone call.

To Implement A Programme - Hire more people and expand the office.

To Activate - To make more copies and add more names to the memo.

To Research - To look for the person who lost the file.

To Put Someone In The Picture - To present a long, confusing and inaccurate explanation to a newcomer.

International Chemicals Plc

Departmental profile.

AN IRISH MOTHER'S LETTER TO HER SON.

Dear Son,

Just a line to let you know that I am still alive. I am writing this letter to you very slowly, as I know that you can't read fast.

About your father, he has got a lovely job now, he has 500 men under him. He is cutting grass in the cemetery.

You won't know the house when you come home, we have moved. There was a washing machine in the new house when we moved in, but it is not working so well. Last week I put 4 shirts in it and pulled the chain, I haven't seen the shirts since.

Your sister Mary had a baby this morning, I haven't found out if it's a boy or a girl, so I don't know if you're an aunt or an uncle. Last week, your uncle Dick was drowned in a vat of whiskey in a Dublin distillery. Some of his pals dived in to try to remove him, but he fought them off bravely. We had him cremated, it took 3 days to put out the fire

Your father did not drink much at Christmas. I put a bottle of castor oil in his beer, it kept him going until New Year's Day.

I went to the Doctor's on Thursday, your father went with me. The Doctor put a small glass tube in my mouth and told me to keep my mouth shut tightly for 10 minutes. Your father wanted to buy the tube from him. It only rained twice last week, the first time for 3 days and then for 4 days.

Did you hear the Gale Warnings on the wireless? It was so windy here on Monday that one of our hens laid the same egg 4 times. We had a nasty letter from that undertaker who buried you grandmother, he said that if we do not pay the last installment within 7 days----up she comes.

As you said you were feeling the cold on the building site I am sending your winter overcoat. To save money on postage, I have cut off those heavy brass buttons, you will find them in the top pocket.

Your Loving Mother.

P.S. I was going to send you £10 for a Christmas present, but then I remembered that I had already sealed the envelope..

THE IDIOT'S DIGITAL CALCULATOR

THE FOLLOWING ARE PURPORTED TO BE ACTUAL STATEMENTS MADE BY CAR DRIVERS IN THEIR REPORTS SUMMARISING THE DETAILS SURROUNDING MOTOR VEHICLE ACCIDENTS. THE DRIVERS WERE ASKED TO DESCRIBE EVENTS IN THE FEWEST POSSIBLE WORDS.

The pedestrian had no idea which direction to run, so I ran over him.

I thought my window was down, but I found out it was up when I put my head through it.

The guy was all over the road, I had to swerve a number of times before I hit him.

Coming home I drove into the wrong house and collided with a tree I don't have.

I was sure the old fellow would never make it to the other side of the road when I struck him.

The other car collided with mine without giving warning of it's intention.

I collided with a stationary truck which was coming the other way.

A truck backed through my windshield into my wife's face.

A pedestrian hit me and went under my car.

I pulled away from the side of the road, glanced at my mother-in-law and headed over the embankment.

In an attempt to kill a fly I drove into a telephone pole.

I had been shopping for plants all day and was on my way home. As I reached an intersection a hedge sprang up, obscuring my vision and I failed to see the other car.

I had been driving for 40 years when I fell asleep at the wheel and had an accident.

I was on my way to the doctor with rear end trouble when my universal joint gave way causing me to have an accident.

As I approached the junction a sign suddenly appeared in a place where no stop sign had ever appeared before.

I was unable to stop in time to avoid an accident.

To avoid hitting the bumper of the car ahead I struck the pedestrian.

My car was legally parked as it backed into the other vehicle.

An invisible car came out of nowhere, struck my car and vanished.

I told the police I was not injured, but on removing my hat found that I had a fractured skull.

I saw a slow moving, sad old gentleman as he bounced off the roof of my car.

The indirect cause of the accident was a little guy in a small car with a big mouth.

I was thrown from my car as it left the road. I was later found in a ditch by some stray cows.

PARKING VIOLATION

COUNTY

AUTOMOBILE
LICENCE NUMBER

AM
PM

DATE

This is not a ticket, but if it were within my power. you would receive two. Because of you Bull Headed, inconsiderate, feeble attempt at parking, you have taken enough room for a 20 mule team, 2 elephants, 1 goat, and a safari of pygmies from the African interior. The reason for giving you this is so that in the future you may think of someone else, other than yourself. Besides I don't like domineering, egotistical or simple minded drivers and you probably fit into one of these categories.

I sign off wishing you an early transmission failure (on the motorway at about 4.30pm). Also may the fleas of a thousand camels infest your armpits.

WITH MY COMPLIMENTS

PARKING VIOLATION

COUNTY

AUTOMOBILE
LICENCE NUMBER

AM
PM

DATE

This is not a ticket, but if it were within my power. you would receive two. Because of you Bull Headed, inconsiderate, feeble attempt at parking, you have taken enough room for a 20 mule team, 2 elephants, 1 goat, and a safari of pygmies from the African interior. The reason for giving you this is so that in the future you may think of someone else, other than yourself. Besides I don't like domineering, egotistical or simple minded drivers and you probably fit into one of these categories.

I sign off wishing you an early transmission failure (on the motorway at about 4.30pm). Also may the fleas of a thousand camels infest your armpits.

WITH MY COMPLIMENTS

PARKING VIOLATION

COUNTY

AUTOMOBILE
LICENCE NUMBER

AM
PM

DATE

This is not a ticket, but if it were within my power. you would receive two. Because of you Bull Headed, inconsiderate, feeble attempt at parking, you have taken enough room for a 20 mule team, 2 elephants, 1 goat, and a safari of pygmies from the African interior. The reason for giving you this is so that in the future you may think of someone else, other than yourself. Besides I don't like domineering, egotistical or simple minded drivers and you probably fit into one of these categories.

I sign off wishing you an early transmission failure (on the motorway at about 4.30pm). Also may the fleas of a thousand camels infest your armpits.

WITH MY COMPLIMENTS

THAT'S NOT MY JOB!

This is a story about four people named: Everybody, Somebody, Anybody and Nobody. There was an important job to be done and Everybody was sure that Somebody would do it. Anybody could have done it, but Nobody did it. Somebody got angry about that, because it was Everybody's job. Everybody thought Anybody could do it, but Nobody realised that Everybody wouldn't do it. It ended up that Everybody blamed Somebody when Nobody did what Anybody could have done.

"ANOTHER MONTH ENDS"

All Targets Met,
All Systems Working,
All Customers Satisfied,
All Staff Eager and Enthusiastic,
All Pigs Fed and Ready to Fly.

BEFORE YOU ASK ME –
THE ANSWER IS

NO

TITLES AVAILABLE FROM PLAYGROUND PUBLISHING

PLEASE SEND ME (POSTAGE FREE):

Men can be such idiots, but you gotta love 'em
Book plus **free Wonderdisk**
@ £4.99 (Free postage)
(The Idiotometer &
When he says... he means...)
ISBN 0-9535987-0-5

Women can be so annoying, but you gotta love 'em
Book plus **free Wonderdisk**
@ £4.99 (Free postage)
(Women-troubleshooting &
When she says... she means...)
ISBN 0-9535987-1-3

The Best of Notice Board Gems	ISBN: 0 9535987 2 1	£3.99
100 Tips for the Frustrated Slimmer	ISBN: 0 9535987 3 X	£1.99
How to break even with Stocks & Shares	ISBN: 0 9535987 4 8	£1.99
The Elderly back at Work	ISBN: 0 9535987 5 6	£2.99
Kcalodisk		£1.99

I have enclosed a cheque/postal order for £....................... made payable to:
Playground Publishing

NAME ....

ADDRESS ....

....

COUNTY .... POSTCODE ....

Fill in the coupon above and send it with your payment to:

Playground Publishing
PO Box 125
Portsmouth
Hampshire
PO1 4PP

Postage free within the United Kingdom

If you wish your purchase to be sent directly to someone else (eg: a Birthday/Christmas/Wedding/Valentines gift), simply fill in their name and address in the coupon above and enclose your cheque/postal order, with your personal message or card, if desired. We will be pleased to send your gift directly to your chosen recipient..

What part of

NO

don't you understand?